A short rock musi
retelling the Biblical story of David and Goliath

David's Rock!
(Goliath's Roll...)

Written and arranged by Sheila Wilson
edited by Alison Hedger

Duration approx. 10 – 15 mins.
(depending on type of performance)

...dedicated to my sister Jill, Dave and Chloë
with much love

Especially suitable for Key Stages 2 + 3 (8 to 13 years)
but will be sung with enthusiasm and enjoyment by younger singers and senior choirs

David's Rock! (Goliath's Roll...) can be performed simply as a series of 5 songs with or without the
narrative. Alternatively the story can be enacted with dialogue added if needed.

The Biblical account of the story, 1 Samuel 17   v.1-50 (Good News Version),
will provide an alternative to the given narrative.

There are three contemporary-style songs, a ballad and a minor key three-part round.

TEACHER'S BOOK
Music and Production Notes
The Pupil's Word Book is published separately GA 10979

1. David Was a Good Man
2. Hallelujah *(3 part round)*
3. Battle Song
4. The Crunch!
5. David's Rock! (Goliath's Roll...)

A matching tape cassette of the music for rehearsals and performances is available,
Order No. GA 10980, Side A with vocals, Side B with vocals omitted

© Copyright Golden Apple Productions
A division of Chester Music Limited
8/9 Frith Street, London W1V 5TZ

Order No. GA 10978 ISBN 0-7119-4715-5

DAVID'S ROCK! (GOLIATH'S ROLL . . .) was written for the children at Marlow Church of England First School, and was then performed by twelve First and Middle school choirs from the Marlow area, as a finale to a joint concert. The children's verdict? "Brilliant! When can we sing it again?"

DAVID'S ROCK! (GOLIATH'S ROLL . . .) can be narrated by one or several narrators, or even recited by the whole choir. If miming or acting is wanted, the narration provides ample self-explanatory stage directions. Dialogue could also be added if required.

Some of the intervals and syncopated rhythms in DAVID'S ROCK! (GOLIATH'S ROLL . . .) are quite complex. But if the songs are sung with gusto and enthusiasm they will be mastered with ease even by young singers, who will have fun getting their tongues around the words!

As a young child I was fortunate to be at a school where we sang some wonderful music, a lot of which I can still recall. If my music and lyrics provide children with that same sense of pleasure and achievement, then I shall be very happy. Music should be fun!

Sheila Wilson

DAVID'S ROCK! (GOLIATH'S ROLL . . .)

NARRATOR/S   Welcome to our classic story,
Told in technicolour glory,
Of the shepherd, of the giant,
One so humble, one defiant.

Before we tell of stone and shield,
Enter David: in a field ...

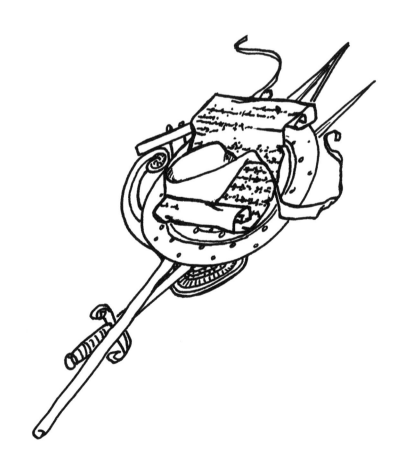

DAVID WAS A GOOD MAN

The use of man here is a colloquialism and does not mean that David was already grown up.

1. David was a good man, he was differ-ent from the rest; God was ve-ry pleased with him be-cause He

knew he was the best! _ 2. He loved to sit and med-

- i - tate, _ and _ to play his lute and sing. _ But

lit - tle did he know _ that _ this shep - herd boy would one day be a king!

_ 3. Come and hear the sto - ry _ a-bout a boy from

far - off Bi - ble lands,__ who trust - ed God and cared

__ for__ his sheep by wrest-ling lions with his bare hands!__

4. Da - vid was a good__ man,__ he was differ - ent from the rest;

__ God had quite a plan__ for__ him be-cause he

6

real - ly was the best, — OH YEAH! You'll see he was the best,

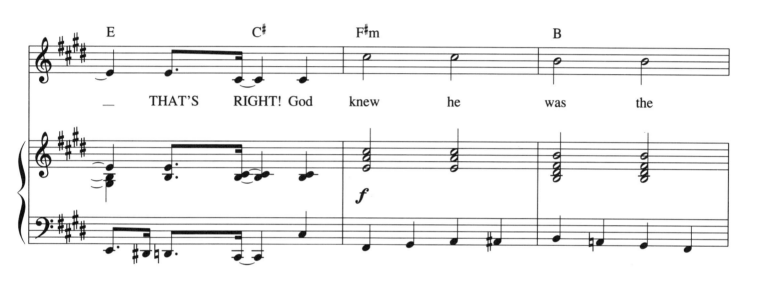

— THAT'S RIGHT! God knew he was the

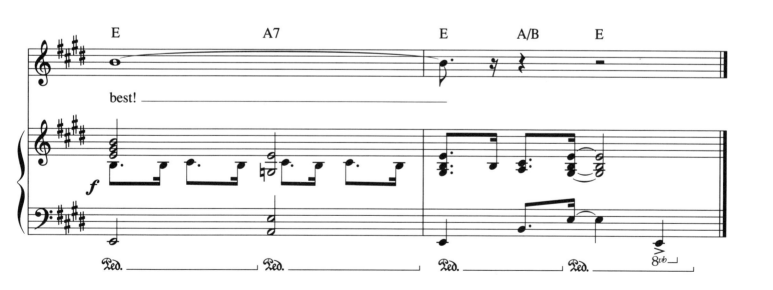

best! ____

NARRATOR/S You'd think that one so strong and sporty,
 Never prone to being naughty,
 Would exercise and train for hours —
 Not lie in fields of grass and flowers,
 Singing songs to his Creator.
 (More of this to follow later.)

 But now: a break from your narrator ...

The round can be short or long. Sheila Wilson suggests the following format:

Group 1 sing the theme through 3 times plus 2 extra Hallelujahs.
Group 2 sing the theme through 3 times plus 1 extra Hallelujah.
Group 3 sing the theme through three times.

All 3 parts will then be singing Hallelujah in unison, ready for the unison CODA.

Substitute the word lute with harp if preferred, as this may be more authentically correct.

2

HALLELUJAH (3 part round)

NARRATOR/S

Not everyone was so ecstatic;
The enemies were problematic.

The Philistines were moving nearer;
The crisis was becoming clearer.

The armies drew their battle line;
And Saul's men prayed for help divine.

3

BATTLE SONG

ways are in Your hand. ___ 2. The en - e - my would des -

- troy us, but in God we place our trust. ___ There's a

sound of bat - tle in the air; ___ please guide our

path, ___ please hear our prayer. The prayer.

11

NARRATOR/S

Just when things could look no worse
Conditions got still more adverse.
The Philistines, they played their ace:
Panic broke out in the place.
"Who" they cried "can save our nation?
Pray to God for inspiration."

For there before their eyes stood one
So mighty, they were overcome.
A giant, yes, no more, no less;
Saul's army trembled in distress.

Then who should chance to pass that way
Than David — come to save the day?
"I'll do it!" said the young sheep farmer,
"But only if you keep that armour!"

So David, there to bring their lunch,
Instead was heading for . . . the crunch!

4
THE CRUNCH!

Fast and exciting ♩ = 152
Each verse slightly louder

1. I - ma-gine, if you can, the un - be - lie - va - ble scene: a
less like - ly duel there nev - er has been: a giant in ar - mour as
big as a house, and Dav - id in a loin cloth, look - ing like a mouse.

2. But 'Ha!' said Dav - id 'for the Lord is on my side! If you had a brain you'd

down went Gol-i-ath like a ton of mixed ce-ment! 'No!' cried the Phil-is-tines, in

un-i-fied la-ment! 'Yo!' sang the Is-rael-ites, *'right be-tween the eyes!' And

Dav-id took his sword and went to claim his prize.

6. The mor-al of this sto-ry is: nev-er back a los-er!

* 'right between the eyes!' may be sung or shouted.

16

NARRATOR/S   Well, our story's nearly over —
              Everybody praised Jehovah,
              Who had given David grace
              To kill that giant face to face.

              But please remember: don't throw stones —
              It's wrong, these days, to shatter bones!

              Instead, in this our final turn,
              Find the lesson you should learn,
              And then, to meet life's final goal,
              Take a Rock and not a Roll ...

5

DAVID'S ROCK! (GOLIATH'S ROLL …)

Lively, fast. ♩ = 144

1. Dav - id had a rock —— well act - ual-ly a stone! It was - n't all that spe - cial, it's the way that it was thrown! He

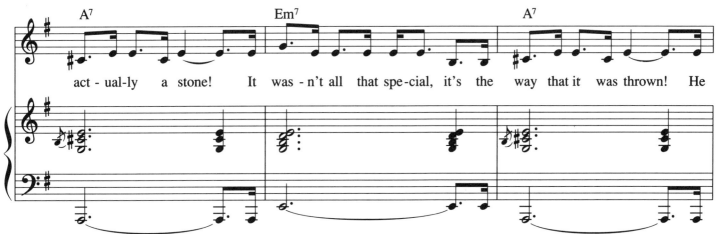

all my soul.___ 2. We all have giants to face in this life:

No-one gets by with - out an-y strife! But re-mem-ber the les-sons_

we have learnt: it's much bet-ter to be on fire than to just get burnt! Oh,

Chorus

Dav - id took a rock!___ Gol - i - ath took a roll! Dav - id served God with

22

* final 'Yeah!' may be sung, cheered or
whispered equally effectively; or omitted!

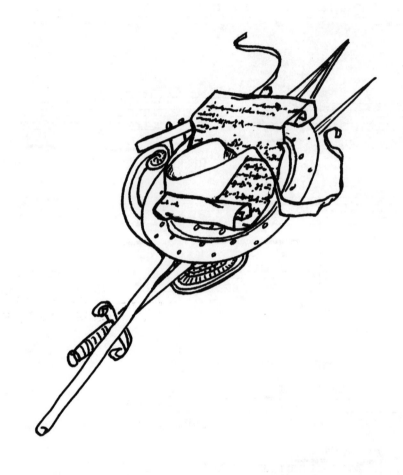